Pass It Down

Five Picture-Book Families Make Their Mark

LEONARD S. MARCUS

Walker & Company

NEW YORK

FOR MY SON, JACOB,

AND IN MEMORY OF MY PARENTS

First published in the United States of America in 2007 by
Walker Publishing Company, Inc.
Distributed to the trade by Holtzbrinck Publishers
For information about permission to reproduce selections from this book, write to Permissions,
Walker & Company, 104 Fifth Avenue, New York, New York 10011

Library of Congress Cataloging-in-Publication Data
Marcus, Leonard S.
Pass it down : five picture book families make their mark / Leonard S. Marcus.
p.   cm.
Includes bibliographical references and index.
ISBN-10: 0-8027-9600-1 • ISBN-13: 978-0-8027-9600-4 (hardcover : alk. paper)
ISBN-10: 0-8027-9601-X • ISBN-13: 978-0-8027-9601-1 (reinforced : alk. paper)
1. Authors, American—20th century—Family relationships. 2. Authors, American—20th century—Biography.
3. Illustrators—United States—Family relationships. 4. Illustrators—United States—Biography.
5. Parent and child—United States—Biography. 6. Children—Books and reading—United States. I. Title.
PS129.M37 2006   813'.5409—dc22 [B]   2006012288

Book design by Claire Counihan
Visit Walker & Company's Web site at www.walkeryoungreaders.com

Printed in China

2 4 6 8 10 9 7 5 3 1

All papers used by Walker & Company are natural, recyclable products
made from wood grown in well-managed forests. The manufacturing processes
conform to the environmental regulations of the country of origin.

Table of Contents

Acknowledgments

I wish to express my thanks to the artists and writers who gave their time and shared their thoughts and memories during the course of the making of this book. For their generous and timely help, thanks also go to: John Barneson of the Kerlan Collection, University of Minnesota; Regina Griffin of Holiday House; Constance Myers; Gloria Jean Pinkney; and Phoebe W. Yeh of HarperCollins. I would also like to express my appreciation for the good work of my editor, Emily Easton, and her assistant, Kate Sullivan; to Claire Counihan for the care and artistry with which she has designed this book; to my agent, George M. Nicholson, for his friendship and guidance; and to my wife and son for their love and support.

# Introduction

Look in the mirror. Who do you see? You, of course, but not you alone. Each of us also carries with us, and within us, all sorts of family traits and resemblances. "What curly hair you have—just like your father's! Ah, but you have your mother's beautiful brown eyes." Grown-ups are always making such remarks to the children they know best. It may seem corny of them to do so. Yet who can blame them? Your face and mine each tell a story that, while mostly our own story, also has much to say about our part in a long, many-stranded tale of generations.

Not all family traits have to do with looks. A child may inherit a tendency to double-jointedness, or an allergy to fish, or a talent for math or music or art. Being born with a talent is just the start, though. Years of study or practice may be needed to make the most of it. Sadly, some people never get the chance. Others are discouraged from pursuing their talent or choose not to do so. It sometimes happens, however, that a child grows up to become an artist or writer. It sometimes even happens that that gifted person's child becomes an artist or writer too. In *Pass It Down*, we meet five such grown sons and daughters who became picture-book creators, like their parents.

These days, there are a great many "picture-book families." But thirty or more years ago, there were hardly any. What brought about this change? After World War II, millions of American soldiers returned home from the battlefield, married, and started families. Tired of war and eager to offer their children safer, happier lives, many of these new parents moved to the suburbs. They gave their children bicycles and other toys and made sure their youngsters got a good education. These same parents—and those who came after them in the 1950s and 1960s—also bought record numbers of books for their children. Because they did so, more artists and writers than ever were needed to create children's books. Making children's books became a more respected profession, and as the children of these writers and illustrators grew up, some of them decided to try their own luck with a paintbrush or pen.

In some ways, the younger generation probably had an easier time of it. While their parents had to blaze new career paths for themselves, didn't they, the children, simply follow their parents' example? Yet none of the stories told here is really that simple. The truth is that growing up is never simple!

As you read about these five families, take a closer look at your family too. Every family has its strengths and talents. What about yours? What do you know about your family's abilities? What more can your parents and relatives tell you? Ask them, and if nothing else, you are bound to hear a good family story or two: A story that may hold a clue to your future. A story that goes with the face you see when you look in the mirror.

THE
Crews and Jonas Family

DONALD CREWS
(born August 30, 1938, Newark, New Jersey)

ANN JONAS
(born January 28, 1932, Flushing, New York)

NINA CREWS
(born May 19, 1963, Frankfurt, Germany)

Nina Crews (left), Donald Crews, and Ann Jonas

Sometimes, not being the eldest child has its advantages. "My father," Donald Crews recalls, "wanted a doctor in the family. He probably would have become one himself had it not been for the way the lives of black people worked when he was young. So a doctor is what my older brother became." Once this happened, Donald and his two sisters felt that a great weight had been lifted off their shoulders. "All our parents asked of us was that we each succeed at *something*."

As a high schooler, Donald had no idea what that something might be. Study art? The thought hardly crossed his mind. For one thing, although his mother was a talented dressmaker and his uncle was an amateur photographer, Donald had never even met a "real" artist. And while art was his favorite class at school, he was absolutely sure that he had no special talent for it.

One of his teachers thought otherwise, however. "Seymour Landsman was quite insistent that several of us apply to art school. He said, 'If you apply, you will get in and you will do well.' You can't let someone down who has that kind of confidence in you."

Donald and his future wife, Ann Jonas, met in 1957 in New York City as fellow students at Cooper Union, a college famous for its School of Art. Ann's family were all amateur artists who built their own furniture and always had some project in the works at home. Her father, a mechanical engineer, would often disappear into the cellar to paint huge, exacting copies of photos from *National Geographic*. Ann's mother painted and played the piano; *her* mother had won a student prize at Cooper Union and had gone on to become a wallpaper and china designer.

At Cooper Union, after trying their hands at "a little bit of everything"— sculpture, painting, architecture, calligraphy, typography—Donald and Ann both realized that their talent lay in graphic design: in the creation of clear, crisp, dramatic visual images that people would notice, quickly grasp, and remember. After four years of study, they both were eager to show the world what they could do.

Ann joined a top-flight design studio run by one of her instructors. Donald landed a job at *Dance* magazine, then went on to a design studio that, like Ann's, was an exciting place to work. In 1962, Donald was drafted into the army and was sent to Germany. Ann moved to Germany to be with him. "An artist," Donald says, "always keeps drawing." When he was not busy doing his job as a military policeman, he worked on his portfolio. He designed a children's ABC book called *We Read: A to Z* (Harper & Row, 1967) as a "way to show people what I could do." In May 1963, the couple's first child, Nina, was born. Donald and Ann returned home to New York with their baby that November. A year later, they had their second daughter, Amy.

With a family to support, Donald and Ann opened a studio in their Greenwich

Nina, 1963.

Village apartment, where, Donald recalls, they designed "lots of book jackets. Then one day an editor asked if I had ever thought of doing a picture book. I showed her *We Read*, and she published it! I did a second book, *Ten Black Dots* (Harper & Row, 1968), to see if the first book had been a fluke. She published that one too. But to earn a living I had to keep designing book jackets. I also illustrated a few science books."

The girls were often around as their parents worked. For Nina, having both parents at home all day meant many things: "not watching as much TV as we wanted," but also

Nina (left) and Amy painting at home, about 1968.

"having free rein of our parents' studio. There were sharp knives to avoid, but for the most part we were allowed to get our hands in things. We drew and painted. Occasionally, we'd be asked to pose or just hold out a finger for Dad to draw. It was expected of us, and it was always fun to be *in* something."

Ann let Nina sit by her drawing table and was usually happy to explain what she was doing and why. Donald was more private about his work. If Nina wanted to know what he was up to, the best way, she found, was to "snoop around the studio" when her father was elsewhere.

Much of the family's life revolved around art.

"Every weekend," Ann remembers with a faint smile, as though unsure whether she and Donald overdid this, "we dragged the girls to another museum."

Donald does not share Ann's doubts. "When we went for long walks, we each carried a sketchbook. At home, we built models and did all kinds of other projects together. Christmas gifts were things that somebody had made: a drawing or photograph or a picture frame—something that you had crafted, never something that you'd bought."

Nina still lights up at the thought of those "projects." "They built our play kitchen. The dollhouse they built us was a brownstone—with an elevator! When I was about eight, I had the Dr. Seuss book *My Book About Me*, which includes a place for writing about your future. I wrote that I was going to become an artist."

Donald, however, was growing tired of chasing down design projects and illustrating other people's books. He yearned for steadier, more satisfying work. "That," he says, "is when I did *Freight Train*" (Greenwillow, 1978).

Everything about the making of *Freight Train* went well. His editor liked the book just as Donald first presented it to her. Nothing had to be changed. Then the excellent reviews poured in.

Behind the clear bright colors and simple bold shapes of *Freight Train* were powerful childhood memories. "Everyone," Donald says, "has trains in their lives. I grew up in Newark, New Jersey, and spent fifteen summers in Florida at my grandmother's farm. As exciting as being at Bigmama's were the trains we rode south to get there and back." As a child, Donald had always wanted, but was never given, a toy train

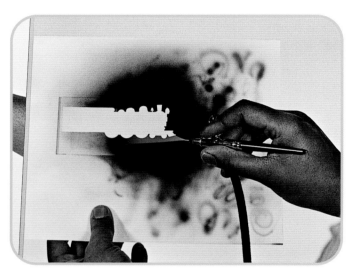

set. Partly with this in mind, he named the imaginary railroad of *Freight Train* the "N & A," after his two daughters.

At fifteen, Nina shared in the excitement when her father won a Caldecott Honor for *Freight Train*. "It was a huge moment in my family's life. We all went to San Antonio to see him accept his award."

Using an "airbrush" (left) Donald streaks and scatters paint to create a feeling of rapid motion in Freight Train *(below).*

Going by cities

Bigmama's house (above)
is depicted in the ink and watercolor sketch
with story notes (left),
and the finished gouache illustration,
(below) featured in Donald's
autobiographical Bigmama's
(Greenwillow, 1991).

"**D**id you see her? Did you see Bigmama?"

We called our Grandma Bigmama. Not that she was big, but she was Mama's Mama.

Every summer we went to see her— Mama, my sisters, my brother, and me. Daddy had to work. He'd come later. It took three days and two nights on the train. Now we were nearly there.

Freight Train (*gouache and airbrush, Greenwillow, 1978*).

Donald has vivid memories of what that time meant to him. "It was the first occasion when either Ann or I had received any recognition for our work." Suddenly, making a living as a picture-book artist seemed possible. With encouragement from Donald and his editor, Ann decided to try making books too.

Ann's first book, *When You Were a Baby* (Greenwillow, 1982), showed how keenly she had observed her daughters' first years. In later books, Nina and Amy became characters. Ann says, "I used to make all the girls' clothes. From the leftover scraps I made a quilt for each of them. At a certain age, Nina, like the main character in *The Quilt* (Greenwillow, 1984), had very dramatic dreams. So, the pieces of the story came together." Ann's *The 13th Clue* (Greenwillow, 1992) recalls a game she organized for her daughters' birthday parties, Spider Web. "You hide small prizes," she explains. "Each is connected to a colored thread. The child has to follow the thread to his or her prize. You end up with a roomful of kids climbing all over each other!" That book also exemplified Ann's fascination with hidden pictures and other visual puzzles.

Donald found his own ways to include his daughters in books. He named two boats in *Harbor* (Greenwillow, 1982) for them; there is also a boat named *Ann*. He made several books about common family activities—sailing, biking, parade watching—both because "we had done them with our kids and because our parents had *not* done

I have a new quilt.

Finished watercolor art for The Quilt, *a story based on details Ann remembered from Nina's childhood.*

them with us. Life was so much harder for our parents. My father had two full-time jobs: a day job and a night job. He slept in small pieces between those jobs."

Donald feels the great gap between his father's life and his own. "He was a general worker who could do a lot of things in an adequate way. I would show him my paintings," he recalls sadly, "but I think they didn't mean much to him." In contrast,

Ink and tempura storyboard study for Ann's Round Trip *(Greenwillow, 1983).*

Donald and Ann saved all their daughters' artwork and encouraged them to enroll in New York City's famed High School of Music and Art: Nina for art, Amy for music.

Then both sisters went to Yale. Nina studied art history at first but then became increasingly passionate about photography. Amy also changed directions, from music to landscape architecture. After college, Nina worked for an animation studio while continuing to take pictures, draw, and think about what kind of artist she wanted to be. Wanting to be helpful, Donald kept suggesting, "Why don't you try a book?" Nina kept resisting.

"Eventually," Nina says, "I had a few half-starts for a children's book that I kept in a bottom drawer. One day when my father was sent a book that he didn't want to illustrate, he suggested to his editor that maybe I could do it instead. So I went in and talked with Susan Hirschman. Susan liked my portfolio but said, "We want you to come up with your own book. Come back with something." I realized I had nothing to lose. About a month later I returned with *One Hot Summer Day*" (Greenwillow, 1995). Hirschman bought it then and there.

Nina had learned a lot about bookmaking from her parents. Like them, she chose a bold, clear typeface, designed big, posterlike page layouts, and told her story in as few words as possible. Unlike them, she created illustrations by combining photography

Photo collage sketch for the illustration in One Hot Summer Day *that accompanies the line,*
"Instead, I stand outside and tease my shadow."

Instead, I stand outside and tease my shadow.

Finished mixed-media photo collage art for One Hot Summer Day.

with collage. At first, she worked more like Donald than Ann, letting no one—certainly not her parents!—see what she was doing. Later, she felt a bit freer about letting them both "into the process." When Ann and Donald finally did see their daughter's first picture book, they were thrilled.

"What pleased us even more," Donald says, was "to see that both our daughters had decided to work for themselves, to be their own boss, to have that freedom. Our grandparents and parents had all worked that way, in bits and pieces. That has been our life and now it is our daughters' life too."

Donald and Ann help celebrate the publication of Nina's first book.

Clement Hurd and Edith Thacher Hurd

Thacher Hurd

THE
Hurd
Family

CLEMENT HURD
(born January 12, 1908, New York, New York;
died February 5, 1988, San Francisco, California)

EDITH THACHER HURD
(born September 13, 1910, Kansas City, Missouri;
died January 25, 1997, Walnut Creek, California)

(JOHN) THACHER HURD
(born March 6, 1949, Burlington, Vermont)

In the home Thacher Hurd grew up in, someone was always painting a picture or writing a story. "We were a little threesome. I was an only child and very close to my parents. In many ways, I saw myself as like them."

In 1949, the year he was born, Thacher's mother, Edith Thacher Hurd, was a thirty-nine-year-old author of more than a dozen picture books and novels. His father, Clement, was forty-one, a war veteran, and the illustrator of nearly twenty books, including several written by his wife. The Hurds lived in an old yellow farmhouse by a river in western Vermont. Thacher, like all his parents' friends, called his father "Clem" and his mother "Posey."

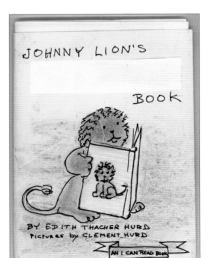

Ink and crayon study for the cover of Johnny Lion's Book *(Harper & Row, 1965),*
one of the fifty-five books that Clem and Posey collaborated on.

Clem in front of the Hurds' Vermont farmhouse, in winter, with the family's German shepherd, Greco, 1947.

The Hurds lived on next to no money. They grew their own vegetables and did most of their own repairs. For a while, they had no indoor plumbing. Most of the time, they enjoyed their rugged, simple existence. In warm weather, Posey took her typewriter outdoors. Clem worked in a rickety shed that he had hauled to the top of a nearby hill. For Thacher, stepping inside that art-filled studio was an "all-senses-at-once experience," a wizard's brew of paint smells, paper textures, tools and brushes, and at the center of it all his tall, rail-thin, slow-moving father silently working.

All this was a far cry from Clem's and Posey's own very proper beginnings. Clem's childhood home was a stately mansion near New York's Central Park. The Hurds were members of New York high society. The future for a child like Clem was as bright with

Posey writing outdoors, Cape Cod, early 1930s.

promise as it was well mapped: Hurd boys attended the best schools, then took their places as Wall Street bankers. Clem's decision, following Yale, to go to Paris and become an artist surprised and worried his parents.

Raised in a comfortable Kansas City, Missouri, household, Posey caused her parents a similar fright when, after graduating from Radcliffe, she enrolled in a teacher-training program that the Thachers and others feared was run by dangerous "radicals." It is true that the Bank Street School in New York's Greenwich Village was a bustling center for "educational experiments," where children aged two through six and future teachers like Posey all learned side by side. Bank Street children were encouraged to speak their minds and not be overly impressed by grown-ups. Neatness and good manners counted for less than knowing what you felt and thought about things. Posey loved being part of a school that showed children so much respect. She loved everything about Bank Street.

It was there that she and a glamorous classmate named Margaret Wise Brown became friends and wrote their first stories for children. "Brownie" was to play a special role in both Clem's and Posey's lives. As an editor a few years later, she published some of Posey's first stories. And before Clem and Posey knew each other, she happened upon some of the artist's playful, colorful paintings, sought him out, and talked him into becoming an illustrator.

Meanwhile, other mutual friends introduced Clem and Posey. The couple married in Manhattan, then moved to Vermont to start a new life far from the social whirl in which Clem no longer felt at home. Although the Hurds and Brownie saw less of each other, they continued to have a great deal to do with one another's careers. Clem illustrated Brownie's *The Runaway Bunny* (Harper & Brothers, 1942) just before leaving to

Posey (left) and Margaret Wise Brown join Clem at the opening of an exhibition of his artwork, New York, 1940.

Ink study for Goodnight Moon. *In the handwritten note at top, Harper's editor Ursula Nordstrom asks Clem to give the cow jumping over the moon a smaller, less conspicuous udder. She adds, "You draw her like a charging bull . . . moo!"*

serve in the army during World War II. On his return three years later, Brownie had the manuscript for *Goodnight Moon* (Harper & Brothers, 1947) waiting for him as a welcome-home present. Posey and Brownie stayed in touch by writing several picture books together, most often sending their unfinished stories back and forth by mail.

In early 1949—the winter of Posey's pregnancy—Clem (in Vermont) and Brownie (in New York) were both hard at work on another book, *My World* (Harper & Brothers, 1949). In the middle of it all, the author, who could be both mischievous and bossy, sent Clem a new version of the manuscript. Brownie, it seemed, had picked out a name for the Hurds' unborn baby. "For Hiram," her dedication read, "when he comes." In the final version of *My World*, published a few months later, the actual dedication read,

For John Thacher Hurd

When he comes

(He's here)

Three years later, in November 1952, Margaret Wise Brown died suddenly, after a brief illness, while traveling in France. She was forty-two. Clem and Posey felt a terrible sadness at her loss. "She was a spark to them," says Thacher, who grew up hearing "Brownie stories." Years and even decades later, his parents remembered her as a friend unlike any other.

In 1954, as Thacher reached kindergarten age, the Hurds moved to northern California for the region's better schools and warmer weather, and to be where Posey's family now lived. Vermont became a place for summer vacations. Perched on a wooded mountainside, the Hurds' new year-round home had a glorious view of San Francisco Bay.

Now when Thacher wandered into Clem's studio, his father might say, "Here's some paper. Here's a pencil." Clem had a self-contained, unhurried manner. When he looked at someone with his intense blue eyes, it felt as though he were gazing out a window from deep inside himself. "Even when he said nothing," Thacher recalls, "the feeling in the room was always clear. You were there and he was there, and you were both working."

Thacher, age seven, and Clem at home, Mill Valley, California, Christmas, 1956.

At Bank Street, Posey and Brownie had tested their stories on the nursery-school children, hoping to learn what interested them and why. Now Posey read her stories to her son and sought his advice. "What's the worst name you can call someone?" she once asked him. Thacher's reply gave her the title she had been looking for: *Last One Home Is a Green Pig* (Harper & Brothers, 1959).

Among the Hurds' artist friends was Don Freeman, the creator of *Corduroy*. "Don," Thacher remembers, "had a big round face. When he came to visit, he brought along his trumpet. He was always smiling. I thought, Wow! Look at the way this person lives. The joy he takes in everything." Freeman, like Clem, made the artist's life seem very appealing.

At seven, Thacher stopped visiting his father's studio, however. "I got self-conscious from being around so much art. As I teenager, I didn't know what I wanted to do. I played in a rock 'n' roll band. I was quite lost in high school."

When Thacher was sixteen, Clem surprised him one day by handing him a manuscript that he had been sent to illustrate. Clem said he had decided not to accept the job. "Here," was all he said to his son. "You try it."

"I worked and worked on it," Thacher remembers. "I don't think I even finished the dummy. Even so, it is wonderful when somebody treats you like that—as an equal. It gives you a confidence that you might otherwise not have had."

Not everything was wonderful, though. "It's a little confusing for a teenager when your parents accept *everything* you do. I couldn't find anything they objected to! When I smoked marijuana briefly, they were *interested*. 'What was it like?' When I made tapes of weird electronic music, they said, 'Fascinating!' My parents had rebelled against their world. But because they were so open to whatever I did, it was really hard to rebel against mine—except by *not* becoming an artist.

"It took college and getting away from home to rediscover art. Suddenly, I said, 'I *like* doing this.'" At first, Thacher painted nothing but landscapes. "Then something sort of turned inside me. The paintings began to feel disconnected from one another. I tried writing a story and realized that making pictures that were linked by a story was what I wanted to do."

At about this time Posey showed Thacher an unfinished story of her own called *Little Dog, Dreaming* (Harper & Row, 1967). She was stuck, she said, and needed ideas.

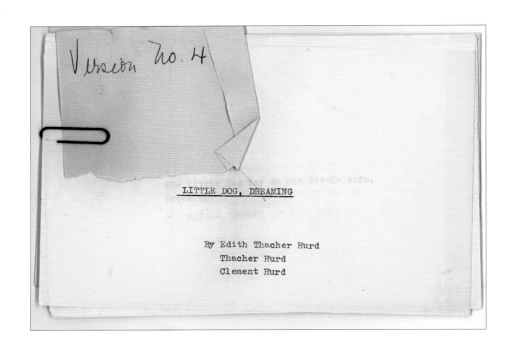

LITTLE DOG, DREAMING

By Edith Thacher Hurd
Thacher Hurd
Clement Hurd

*Title page for the fourth of eight
saved drafts of the text for
Little Dog, Dreaming.*

When *Little Dog, Dreaming* was published with illustrations by Clem, Thacher's name appeared as its coauthor.

A keenly observant person with a dry sense of humor, Posey had a good teacher's knack for explaining things. "I would show her my first dummies, and she would help with story lines, plotting, even getting the dummy to look presentable.

"My first books were in my parents' and Brownie's mold: quiet and poetic. Then it came time to do something different, and I wanted to make books with adventure, mystery, and humor." *Hobo Dog* (Scholastic, 1980) was the first of these. Not long afterward, Thacher had fun creating a character named Farmer Clem who lived on a farm like the Hurds' Vermont summer home. In *The Pea Patch Jig* (Crown, 1986), *Blackberry Ramble* (Crown, 1989), and *Tomato Soup* (Crown, 1991), a family of mice lead busy, eventful lives that go unnoticed by the farmer. "The baby mouse is a version of me, doing the mischief that I, as such a good kid, had always been afraid to do."

By the time Thacher's career took off in the 1980s, both Posey and Clem had retired. One reason they could do so was that *Goodnight Moon*, after growing steadily more popular over the years, had become one of the bestselling children's books of all time.

"Clem got enormous pleasure from its belated success," Thacher says. "He would write the sales figures on tiny pieces of paper and show them to me. It was more difficult for my mother. People would think that she had written *Goodnight Moon* and

Ink and watercolor study for The Pea Patch Jig.

would want to talk to her about it." Even so, she took delight in telling stories about Brownie, "our lovely and creative friend," from whom both she and Clem had learned so much.

In retirement, Posey still enjoyed helping her son polish his latest dummy. Clem helped too, though not with advice. "I don't know quite how he did it," Thacher says. "There was a certain way he would smile, a certain body language. He radiated love. Most of us are so focused on saying the right words. Clem had a way of just *being there*."

The Pea Patch Jig
(*ink and watercolor, Crown,* 1986).

Walter Dean Myers and Christopher Myers

THE
Myers
Family

WALTER DEAN MYERS
(born August 12, 1937, Martinsburg, West Virginia)

CHRISTOPHER MYERS
(born October 17, 1974, Astoria, New York)

"We lived on the cusp," Walter Dean Myers says of the Jersey City home where his son, Christopher, grew up during the 1970s. "On one side of our house, the neighborhood was all white. On the other side it was predominantly black. Christopher was a mixed-race kid. Because he could read at four, he started school early. His classmates were all two years older than him. He was not a good athlete. So he was pushed around a bit in school."

"Classmates looked at me," Christopher Myers recalls, "as if I had three heads."

Walter, the author of *Bad Boy* (Amistad/HarperCollins, 2001), grew up knowing a lot about not getting along well at school. Raised by foster parents in the economically depressed Harlem of the 1940s, he was a restless, inward-looking, overtall boy with a lisp and a serious tendency to take a fist to anyone who made fun of him. His foster parents worked long hours to make ends meet. Although genuinely concerned about his welfare, they were often unaware when their son skipped entire weeks of school.

Walter was lucky enough to have a few teachers who, despite his record as a troublemaker, wanted to help him. Some gave him books that made him hungry for more books. Reading—and by middle school, writing—became his life preservers.

Christopher, age two.

As a teenager, as Walter became more aware that "blacks did not have the same chances as whites," his doubts about the future multiplied. It never occurred to him that he might one day write a book. Even as a first-time author, as a man in his thirties, Walter says, "I didn't think I was going to have a career. I thought that maybe I would get published occasionally." After years of earning his living as an editor, Walter became a full-time writer in 1977. He was forty. Christopher was three.

"I'm an early riser, and when Christopher was going to day care," Walter recalls of that time, "I'd finish work in the late morning and pick him up, and we would hang out together in the afternoon, which was very cool. We talked, very often solving the world's problems. I enjoyed his company.

"We read together: first comics, which had been forbidden to me as a child, and *Reader's Digest*, because we both loved jokes. Later, we read poetry." On weekends, father and son took the train into Manhattan and headed for their "Golden Triangle"—their three favorite bookstores, including one called Forbidden Planet— from which they always returned with armloads of books.

Walter, as his foster father had done with him, often told Christopher farfetched stories that he presented as true. Christopher remembers: "I wouldn't eat Brussels sprouts for years because of a story he told me. I had asked him, 'What *are* they? They're so odd-looking.' He responded with a long, involved story about a war we had fought in the sixties with a race of very small aliens. Brussels sprouts were the aliens' leftover heads. I was glad to find this out because now I knew why I was *never* going to eat Brussels sprouts again."

This was not the only way that Walter taught his son not to believe everything he heard or read. "Pop," Christopher says, "would go through my school history texts and write corrections in them. When a book referred to 'bringing the slaves from Africa,' he would cross that out, wanting to be sure I understood that African *people* had been *enslaved*. I was a good student, but I learned early on that education didn't necessarily happen in school. And I learned from Pop that books did not come down from on high: that people wrote them, and that there was work for me to do."

Christopher was drawing two hours a day by the time he was nine. Walter takes no credit for this. "His mom, who paints, must have noticed he had talent, because I didn't! Connie would put his drawings up on the refrigerator or the wall. At about ten, he won some contests, but I still wasn't paying much attention. Then he had a picture published in a children's magazine. I saw it—a drawing of an antelope or something—and said, 'That's really *good*.'"

Connie took Christopher to museums and comic book fairs and once, on his birthday, on a tour of Marvel Comics. Walter, meanwhile, involved his wife and their son in every aspect of his work.

Christopher remembers: "My father wrote ten pages a day. When he was done, he would come down and have me read it out loud so that my mother and he could talk about it."

As a teenager, Christopher accompanied his mother to the library to help research Walter's books. "Digging up information about African-American history strengthened my link to my cultural background," Christopher says. "I also realized that there were true stories worth finding, and that it was possible to unearth them."

Christopher and Walter at an event celebrating the publication of Harlem, *Stapleton Branch Library (Staten Island), New York Public Library, May 1998.*

When Walter discussed a new publishing contract with his wife, he encouraged Christopher to join in the discussion. "He wanted me even at nine and ten to see," Christopher says, "that a contract is part of the process by which books are made."

What Christopher most wanted, however, was to draw the pictures for his father's books. He recalls the first time he and his father talked about this: "I was ten and reading fantasy novels when Pop said one day, 'Let's do a fantasy together. What would you like to see in it?'

'How about a black unicorn?' I said.

'That's cool,' he said. 'What's his problem? We need to give him a problem.'" Years passed before Walter was able to answer his own question and finish *Shadow of the Red Moon* (Scholastic, 1995). Christopher, then a college student, illustrated the book, finally getting his wish.

Collage self-portrait made by Christopher, age fourteen.

In the meantime, Walter occasionally put his son in a book: "He is T. J., the major character in *Me, Mop, and the Moondance Kid* (Delacorte, 1988). Christopher was playing Little League baseball then and thought he was pretty good. You know, kids' imaginations! He is also in *The Beast* (Scholastic, 2003). When Christopher was at Brown University, he would come home all full of himself. Looking around our neighborhood, he would give me very disparaging reports. That really upset me. I had wanted him to go to a good school. At his age, I hadn't been able to go to college. But I did not want him to turn his back to the neighborhood. So I was upset—until we went around together, and I saw that he was right. Many of his friends had fallen by the wayside, were drifting into some bad kind of life. Christopher wondered what had happened to them. I began to wonder too. That became *The Beast*."

In all, Christopher illustrated two of his father's books while still at college: *Shadow of the Red Moon* and a picture book called *Harlem* (Scholastic, 1997). Both times, Walter

Harlem: A Poem *(mixed-media collage, Scholastic, 1997).*

suggested the idea and both times, Walter says, "the publisher was not happy about it. It gets too personal. They did not want to have to turn down my son. So Christopher did sample illustrations and had them accepted. When *Harlem* won a Caldecott Honor, everyone began saying, 'Father, son; father, son!' It's been much easier since then."

In 1999, Christopher launched his solo career with *Black Cat* (Scholastic, 1999), a haunting picture book that, aptly, traces the wanderings of a lone cat as he makes a place for himself in a big and not always welcoming city. That same year, he illustrated his father's powerful novel about urban teenage violence, *Monster* (Amistad/HarperCollins, 1999). The next picture book Walter wrote for Christopher to illustrate was about the blues. As in the past, Christopher showed his father the artwork for *Blues Journey* (Holiday House, 2003) only after he had finished it.

Walter says, "I think he's still afraid of that father-and-son thing, the father as

HOLIDAY HOUSE

425 Madison Avenue, New York, NY 10017
212-688-0085   FAX 212-421-6134

August 13, 2000

Mr. Walter Dean Myers
2543 Kennedy Dr.
Jersey City, NJ 07304

RE: blue's journey

Dear Walter:

I am very, very sorry to have taken so long getting my comments back to you. I was still sick (8 weeks now) and it threw me further behind. And I wanted to do some reading, so I wouldn't mortify myself by asking who Skippy is!

I noticed he no longer makes an appearance – is that for your ignorant editor's sake?

You are great – I just clap after some of the lines. You've captured the humor, pathos, sexiness, despair– the spirit of the blues. And it's a pretty show off-y piece in the best way-- playing around with different blues forms – showing that you can do it all– just like a musician should.

I began doing page breaks, but then realized I wanted to talk to you and Chris about the length. Did we want to have printed ends?

Remember my suggestion, which you had sounded interested in, about a sort of metaphoric map of the blues? Somewhere in the book… Of course, maybe Christopher wasn't interested in it.

Also, I wondered whether you might consider an inventive journey into lexicography? Perhaps a spread at the end, or endpapers, pointing out some of the traditional images and terms of the blues that you've used here. (Crossroads, hound dog, crow, etc.) This doesn't have to be done in a stuffy way-- it could be original and fascinating.

But I needed to know that so I would know how long the book would be.

The call and response stanza – I wasn't sure whether that worked either where it was placed, or maybe it sounds too contemporary?? What do you think?

At the risk of sounding like a complete Puritan, I think the stanza about bringing hot coffee, and a body like a guitar might not be perfect for a juvenile book. Maybe, the entendres aren't double enough?? And please don't replace it with a hambone, sugar, or any of the other traditional gifts!!

I know that sex is essential to the blues, but see if you can cloak it a bit more!

On the beautifully written "note" at the back. For some reason, my mind keeps having a problem going to the cities first, and then down to the country. It must be my historian's mind – locked in chronology. You can probably convince me, but would you take another look??

Also, since the blues have to be useful, I was thinking that the note should be too.

Would you consider adding a few basic facts – in your adroit and subtle way, naturally-- about the traditional structure of the blues?

I was thinking of 12 bar, 3 chords, flattened notes, the basics.   It is amazing (sort of Zen-like) that in such a tight structure, there is *such* a variety of sounds and feelings…

This is me being Willis Reed – you know musically what the blues are, but lots/most of the readers won't really.

All my best,

Regina Griffin

Letter to Walter from editor Regina Griffin, with comments on the manuscript of Blues Journey.

judge." Christopher agrees. "If we talked about it sooner, he might make some comment that would 'get into my head.'" But Christopher is not alone in his worries. Walter adds, "We're both nervous because we both want to hold up our end. We feed on the tension."

"Writing *Blues Journey*," Walter recalls, "was easy for me. I am comfortable with the blues lyric form." For Christopher, however, illustrating his father's poems was anything but easy. "I wanted the images to tell a parallel story, not just link one-to-one to the poems."

Christopher remembers, "I struggled with the poem about 'strange fruit,' wondering how to deal with lynching in a picture book. I didn't want to show the horror of lynching. And I didn't want to present black children with a picture of

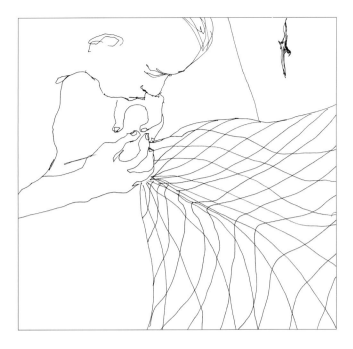

Pencil study by Christopher for Blues Journey.

black people as victims. Finally, I decided on an image of a child protester, to show something that a child could do."

Walter admired his son's artwork but was puzzled by "a picture with a fisherman and his net. It didn't seem to go with any of the poems. So I wrote another poem to go with the image.

"Years earlier," Walter says, "I learned about the power of images from Christopher. My wife and I collect photographs. We have about ten thousand, most of black life between 1855 and 1940. I began collecting them when I was teaching a writing workshop for middle-school kids in Jersey City. Christopher, who was thirteen, was there too, drawing the illustrations for their yearbook. The kids would write such negative things about themselves, nasty racial remarks like: 'You're so black, you're toasty.' I thought, whatever happened to 'Black

Finished art in mixed media on brown-bag paper for the fisherman poem in Blues Journey.

blues journey

by Walter Dean Myers
illustrated by Christopher Myers

Blues Journey (*mixed media on brown-bag paper, Holiday House, 2003*).

is beautiful?' I wanted to do something about it, and because the kids were so into the images Christopher was making, I thought, let's bring in some photographs. That experience also led to *Brown Angels*" (HarperCollins, 1993).

Looking back, Walter says, "I think that probably I have gained more from Christopher than he has from me. I've published more than eighty books. After a while you repeat yourself. But with Christopher's constant push toward innovation, I feel refreshed."

When Walter first saw the art for *Blues Journey*, he paid Christopher his version of a high compliment: "If I'd known you were going to do something that good," he told his son, "I would have written it better."

By now, Christopher usually knows when his father is teasing. "Oftentimes," he says, "he'll call me. I'll pick up the phone and he'll say, 'Why you talking on the phone?' And I'll say, 'Because you called me.' 'Well I'm working,' he'll say. 'I can't talk to people like you!' Then he'll hang up the phone. In that joking way of his there's also a seriousness—the idea that he's always working, and that my life has to be about always working too."

Brian Pinkney

THE
Pinkney
Family

JERRY PINKNEY
(born December 22, 1939, Philadelphia, Pennsylvania)

(JERRY) BRIAN PINKNEY
(born August 28, 1961, Boston, Massachusetts)

Jerry Pinkney

Some children know, early on, what they want to do for the rest of their lives. Jerry Pinkney knew he was going to draw. In the African-American section of north Philadelphia where he grew up during the 1940s and 1950s, few children would have imagined such a future for themselves.

For one thing, no artists lived in the Pinkneys' working-class neighborhood. Jerry's father sometimes painted houses to earn money. But work for him and most everyone the Pinkneys knew was about making a living. Later, as a high school student at a trade school in another part of town, Jerry did meet an African-American art teacher who took an interest in him. But as graduation neared, the school's white guidance counselor made a point of discouraging Jerry and his fellow classmates of color from trying for art school scholarships. (Jerry applied for one, anyway, and received a full scholarship to the Philadelphia Museum College of Art.) Although segregation was illegal in Philadelphia, African Americans were also made to feel unwelcome in the elegant part of town where most of the city's great art museums were located. Despite his passion for drawing, Jerry completed high school without once setting foot in a museum or gallery.

At home, Jerry's mother always had a good word to say about his drawing. His father, who was a distant, practical-minded handyman, at least never *discouraged* him. When Jerry was eleven, a famous Philadelphia cartoonist named John J. Liney saw him out sketching one day and complimented him on his drawing ability. He invited Jerry to visit his studio. Being taken seriously by a real artist meant a lot to him. But that one experience—and the solid art skills training he received at his vocational high school—was about all the help he received before college. Later, when he became a father, Jerry was determined that his own children would have a better introduction to art. The effort began early.

"In every house we lived in," Jerry recalls, "we tried to create a common space with worktables, art supplies—and no television. In that room, the children could do anything they wanted. I made a point of not hanging any of my work in the house. I didn't want them to be overshadowed. The house belonged to all of us."

In 1960, while still a college student, Jerry married his high school sweetheart, Gloria Maultsby. Soon after their daughter, Troy, was born, the Pinkneys moved to Boston. Over the next few years, three more children arrived: Brian, Scott, and Myles. While Gloria cared for the family, Jerry worked at a greeting card company before joining Barker-Black, a design studio, where his assignments included illustrating several children's books, starting with *The Adventures of Spider: West African Folktales* (Little, Brown, 1964), retold by Joyce Cooper Arkhurst.

Picture books played only a small part in the Pinkneys' own home life, however, and with good reason. "We were caught up in the civil rights movement," Jerry recalls, "and we became aware of the lack of picture books that mirrored the lives of people of African descent." A gifted storyteller, Gloria preferred telling stories to reading books aloud, anyway. But as Jerry met other African-American artists living in Boston and came to see himself as a member of their community, he began to look for illustration projects that reflected his own growing interest in African-American culture.

A turning point came when Jerry volunteered to work at the Elma Lewis School of Fine Arts, a cultural center founded to provide Boston's African-American children and their families with enriching experiences in the arts.

Gloria says, "We enrolled all our children in the center's after-school program, which included classes in drama, dance, and art, all taught by talented professionals. I took a dance class too. It was wonderful for all of us."

Brian, age ten.

The Pinkneys paid close attention to their children as they grew in different directions. "Whenever one chose an interest," says Jerry, "we tried to feed that interest by giving them the materials they needed." Gloria adds, "From early on, Brian made nearly all his own toys, turning pipe cleaners into stick-figure people, rockets, entire cities." Later, a supply of balsa wood, good for use in model building, became Brian's idea of a "cool" present. When at eleven or twelve Myles showed an interest in photography, his parents gave him a camera.

The children were still young when Jerry began to work at home. As Brian recalls, "We weren't allowed to visit him in his studio except after school, when he would like us to come in and talk about our day. The big thing was to model for him, which I found fun. My mother had costumes and would dress us up. She would often model too. Once my sister wasn't at home when my father needed a girl model, so he gave me a wig and dressed me up as a girl. That *wasn't* fun! But I did it."

"As a model, Brian was patient and was very sensitive to what his dad was trying to do," Gloria remembers.

"Scott," on the other hand, "was more difficult," according to Jerry, "always wanting his own way. I think that is why he became an art director!" Jerry continues.

"All of the children drew well and could easily have gone into illustration. But they were each looking to find their own way." Troy, like her mother, turned to handicrafts and became a skilled weaver and later also a recreational therapist. Myles became a photographer.

Brian holding a mailing tube in place of a saxophone as he poses for Jerry for Half a Moon and One Whole Star *by Crescent Dragonwagon (Macmillan, 1986).*

Finished art in watercolor and pencil for Half a Moon and One Whole Star, *based on the photo on page 34.*

Brian, more than the others, watched his father. He was determined to draw—and be—like Jerry. When Brian was about eight, the residents of their Boston neighborhood decided to fix up the local playground. Jerry organized the neighborhood children to help him paint a big mural. As a fourth grader the following year, Brian, "the class artist," painted a mural of his own on his classroom wall.

The next year, the Pinkneys moved to a small town north of New York City. As Brian's passion for drawing continued to grow, Gloria recalls, she and Jerry "took the closet in the room the three boys shared, and made it into a studio for him. It was a large closet. I moved everything out. We got Brian a desk—just like Jerry's, but smaller—and said that that was his space where he could close the door and draw." By high school, Brian was determined to do "just what my father was doing as an artist—everything!—including advertising, books, and magazine illustration."

Jerry's artwork was now increasingly in demand. During the 1970s, he created a series of calendars picturing the unsung lives of the black cowboys of the American Wild West, illustrated a dozen children's books, and drew the covers for Virginia

Hamilton's first Newbery Honor winner, *The Planet of Junior Brown* (Macmillan, 1971) and Mildred D. Taylor's Newbery Medal winner, *Roll of Thunder, Hear My Cry* (Dial, 1976). Starting in 1978, he designed each of the U.S. Post Office's first nine annual Black Heritage Month commemorative stamps.

Brian illustrated his first picture book, *The Story Teller* (text by Derrick Gantt, Songhai Press, 1983), just after graduating from the Philadelphia Museum College of Art, the same school his father had attended. Although Brian himself was unhappy with his first effort, it showed Jerry that his son "already understood how to put a book together." His second book, *Shipwrecked on Mystery Island*, by Roy Wandelmaier (Troll, 1985), followed two years later. Then a publisher asked Jerry to illustrate a picture book by Robert D. San Souci called *The Boy and the Ghost* (Simon & Schuster, 1989). Jerry turned down the project but told the publisher, "I know someone else who I think could do it"—Brian, of course. Jerry no longer remembers why he did not want the project for himself, but Brian recalls that Jerry told him that it was because he could not picture the story's ghost. In an amusing twist, Brian had Jerry model for the ghost!

The Boy and the Ghost still left Brian feeling unsatisfied. Illustrated in watercolor, a medium in which his father was considered a master, the art struck him as too similar to Jerry's work. For Brian, this was a touchy, difficult time. Gloria remembers this "important time in Brian's life" well. "Brian's name is really Jerry: Jerry Brian Pinkney. When he began illustrating books, he decided not to use the 'Jerry' anymore and to sign his name 'J. Brian Pinkney.' Even so, people still confused him with his father."

Disturbed by this, Brian returned to art school—an unusual choice for a published illustrator with steady work. In a class where students were urged to "play" with new techniques and materials, Brian made a scratchboard drawing one day of a boy on a bicycle, and he knew quite suddenly that he had found a way to make pictures that was really his own.

"I was in the middle of illustrating *The Ballad of Belle Dorcas* (text by William H. Hooks, Knopf, 1990) in watercolor," he recalls. "But after that experience, I couldn't go back to watercolor. So I started the book over and illustrated *The Ballad of Belle Dorcas* in scratchboard. People said: 'Why did you do that? So you wouldn't look like your father anymore?' I said, 'I did it to look more like me. The other stuff is me also, but this is *more* me.'"

Then a scowling head, with hair and beard red as flame and eyes like blazing coals, dropped *Thunk!* into the fireplace ashes.

Right away the body of the man, or ghost, or whatever it was, picked up the head from the hearth, brushed it off, and set it squarely on its shoulders.

"Now," roared the figure, hands on hips, "What do you say?"

"Do you want some soup?" asked Thomas, who wouldn't let his courage or his manners fail him, "There's still a little left in the pot, and you're welcome to share it."

Pencil study (above) and finished watercolor and pencil art (below) by Brian for
The Boy and the Ghost, *for which Jerry posed as the ghost.*

Finished scratchboard illustration for The Ballad of Belle Dorcas.

The Ballad of Belle Dorcas was also the first book he signed "Brian Pinkney." That same year, Jerry illustrated three books: *Further Adventures of Uncle Remus* (retold by Julius Lester, Dial, 1990); *Home Place* (text by Crescent Dragonwagon, Macmillan, 1990); and *Pretend You're a Cat* (text by Jean Marzollo, Dial, 1990); and he won his second Caldecott Honor for *The Talking Eggs* (text by Robert D. San Souci, Dial, 1989).

When Brian and Jerry look back at the start of their careers, they inevitably see very different beginnings. "I had so many opportunities," Brian realizes. "It was very cool." Jerry's opportunities had been harder won. "After *Mirandy and Brother Wind*" (text by Patricia C. McKissack, Knopf, 1988), the book for which Jerry received his first Caldecott Honor, "the awards came quickly. But there had been

SWISH! SWISH!

It was spring, and Brother Wind was back. He come high steppin' through Ridgetop dressed in his finest and trailing that long, silvery wind cape behind him.

SWOOSH! SWOOSH! SWOOSH!

89

Pencil study for Mirandy and Brother Wind.

more than twenty years leading up to that time when there was no great market for the kind of work that interested me."

But every artist has some struggle. First, Brian needed to be like his father; then he needed to be unlike him. Now he and his wife, Andrea, a writer and publisher with whom he often collaborates on books, have two young children of their own. Brian believes that at least one of them may have the talent and drive to become an artist too. If she does so, what might it be like for her as one of a famous family's third generation of artists? It would be exciting, for sure, but probably not always easy to follow in so many illustrious footsteps.

For a long time, Jerry thought of the artist's life he made for himself as a very different kind of life from the one his father had led. Yet family resemblances run

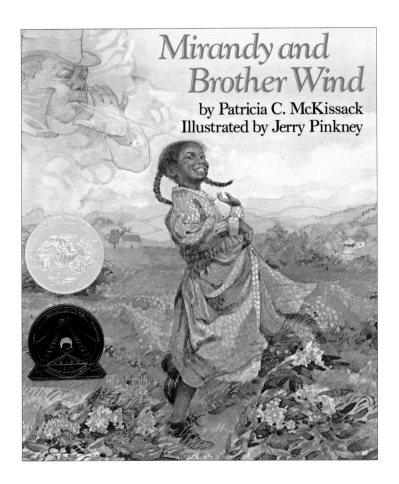

Mirandy and Brother Wind, *text
by Patricia McKissack (watercolor
and pencil, Knopf, 1988).*

deep and can sometimes surprise. Looking back now, he sees that in some ways he and his father were much more alike than he realized. "My father," he says, "loved wood and carpentry. What I remember most fondly about him is the joy he took in the things he made. If you look at how I work, it's very much like woodworking. I need to touch things. I approach my work as a craft. He worked with tools and wood. I work with a pencil or brush and paper. But it's one and the same."

THE Rockwell Family

Anne Rockwell (left) and Lizzy Rockwell

HARLOW ROCKWELL
(born December 11, 1910, Buffalo, New York; died April 7, 1988, Greenwich, Connecticut)

ANNE ROCKWELL
(born February 8, 1934, Memphis, Tennessee)

LIZZY ROCKWELL
(born August 30, 1961, New York, New York)

Harlow Rockwell

"Some of my strongest childhood memories," Lizzy Rockwell says, "are of my mom and dad working together. They had a tiny studio—almost all windows—off the dining room, in the heart of our house. The French doors were always left open. It was the first place we went when we came home from school. To a small child it was fascinating."

Lizzy's mother, Anne Rockwell, remembers those long-ago afternoons too, but differently. To her, the children's return meant time to rinse out her watercolor brush and wipe her drawing pen clean for the day: time to go back to being a mother. "I've never been very good at doing two things at once," Anne says with a laugh.

Harlow Rockwell, an advertising artist, was used to office noise and clatter. But he had never gotten used to letting other people look over his shoulder as he worked. Sharing a studio was hard for him. Eventually, he moved his drawing table to a separate studio in their yard.

Anne had been twenty-one when she married Harlow Rockwell in 1955, an artist in his forties, in New York City. To help pay the rent, she took a job as a secretary.

After hours, she did her real work, painting and sculpting. Three years later, when the couple's first child, Hannah, was born, Anne went shopping for bedtime books one day and was astonished by the art she found in picture books by Maurice Sendak and others. "Until then," Anne says, "I had never thought about being an illustrator. But when I saw those exciting books, I realized, *this* is what I should be doing." She wrote stories in order to have something to illustrate.

Once a week, Harlow looked after Hannah—and then also their second child, Lizzy—while Anne made the rounds of publishers. Remarkably, she sold her first book, *Paul and Arthur Search for the Egg* (Doubleday, 1964), to the very first editor who saw it. Then Anne got a taste of failure. Twenty-two publishers turned down her second book, *Gypsy Girl's Best Shoes* before she finally sold it to Parents Magazine Press in 1966. Publishers, it seemed, felt more comfortable with a children's story about an egg hunt than they did about one that described the life of a poor girl growing up in New York City.

In 1967, when their third child, Oliver, was two, the Rockwells moved to Connecticut. Always a keen observer, Anne watched with amazement as her three children grew and changed. Each of them, she realized, went about life in a completely different way. When Hannah first talked, for example, "getting each word right was what mattered to her.

"But Lizzy was a babbler. Babblers mimic the sounds they hear other people making because they're so eager to join in the conversation.

Lizzy, age eight, and her brother, Oliver, four, on the island of Ischia, in southern Italy.

It is my father's toolbox.

Finished watercolor art for The Toolbox.

"Then came Oliver. He would go for weeks without saying anything and then surprise us by coming out with a very well-thought-out phrase that was more like poetry than prose. That's how *The Toolbox* (Macmillan, 1971; Walker, 2004) got started. Olly loved his father's toolbox. One day he said to us: 'It's dark brown where hands have touched it.'" *The Toolbox* was the fourth book by Anne that Harlow illustrated. Lizzy's parents were becoming a well-known picture-book team. At the same time, Anne still enjoyed working alone on some books and writing or illustrating books with others.

Reading to her children taught Anne to see books differently. At first, Lizzy's fondness for *Papa Small*, by Lois Lenski (Oxford, 1951; Random House, 2004), for instance, really puzzled her. Anne could remember *dis*liking other similar books by Lenski as a little girl! Finally, she asked Lizzy why she liked it. "Because Papa Small is *so* beautiful," replied her daughter. Anne remained unsatisfied. She grumbled to herself: "*What* beauty is she talking about? Is it the beauty of little heads drawn perfectly round with a compass? Or is it that this is the story of a real daddy doing

The Small family gardens together in Papa Small, *by Lois Lenski.*

the things that real daddies do in the morning: shaving, getting in his car?" Anne could recall watching, wide-eyed, as her own father shaved in the mirror every morning. With that memory freshly fixed in her mind, Lizzy's feeling for the book suddenly became clear to Anne.

Lizzy now believes she was so taken with *Papa Small* because "the members of the Small family garden together, carry in the groceries together, sweep the floor together. They get along! It was very much the way our family lived."

Anne's early home life in Tennessee could hardly have been less like the Smalls'. Her parents divorced when she was seven. From then on Anne and her two younger sisters moved with their restless mother from state to state. Torn between the wish to raise her daughters properly and vague dreams of becoming a writer, Anne's mother enrolled the girls in a series of boarding schools, taking off for long periods without telling anybody where she was going. Finally, their mother abandoned the girls for good, and Anne and her sisters had to be put in the care of foster parents.

Throughout those hard years, Anne found comfort and pleasure in books. She wrote stories too, even though she became convinced early on that she was not much good at it. *Good* writers, Anne believed, wrote stories about elves and fairies. That, anyway, was what all the other girls she knew wrote about. "I was only interested in writing about the real world." Back in Tennessee, when her father was still living at home, Anne "would take his shirt cardboard every day and do a comic strip on it." Anne's story was always about "what had gone on that day on my street and in my family."

Lizzy's childhood, while far more like the Smalls' than her mother's, was still not simple. "I was in a house," she recalls, "where everybody was so talented that I didn't notice my own talent particularly. My sister, with whom I was close, was such a good artist that when a teacher praised my artwork, I would think, you should see what Hannah can do! I imagined that Hannah would become a famous artist one day and that I might grow up to raise a family and teach. Even so, I continued to draw."

In high school, Lizzy wanted to draw pictures that looked real. "It felt magical that, with shading, I could make a flat piece of paper look like it had something on it you could touch." Art was becoming a bigger part of her life. After school, she helped out in her mother's studio. "Then at Connecticut College I made large abstract paintings and drawings, and I found that I loved talking about pictures as well as making them." She considered becoming an art historian but realized she did not want to keep studying for several more years. "That was when my dad said, 'Well, why aren't you going to become an illustrator?' And I said, 'Why aren't I?'"

Harlow and Anne worried about their daughter, though. "Lizzy had always been happiest among people," says Anne, "and we both knew how lonely it could be, living with a book by yourself for months."

After college, Lizzy returned to her parents' home for a time, then moved to New York, where she freelanced, designing book jackets and illustrating for magazines. She married an artist and sometimes collaborated with him on projects. Then, in 1988, after a long illness, Harlow Rockwell died. On his drawing table he had left the unfinished art for the third in a series of four picture books about the seasons, written by Anne.

I looked into the yellow forsythia bush, but my robin wasn't there.

Finished watercolor art by Harlow for My Spring Robin.

Finished watercolor art by Lizzy for My Spring Robin.

At the Beach (Macmillan, 1987) and *The First Snowfall* (Macmillan, 1987) had already been published. Knowing that he would not live to finish *My Spring Robin* (Macmillan, 1989), Harlow told Lizzy that he thought she could complete the book. "Our publisher," Anne recalls, "felt timid about letting Lizzy take over." Lizzy, after all, had never illustrated a book. "But to me it seemed like such a natural progression."

Lizzy had doubts of her own. "It was the family business," she explains, "and often you go into the family business a little bit cautiously." Complicating matters was the requirement that the pictures be drawn in her father's style rather than her own. "But I saw that *My Spring Robin* needed to be finished and that finishing it was a family responsibility. I approached the work with a great sense of pride." Then Lizzy illustrated the fourth book, *Apples and Pumpkins* (Macmillan, 1989). In an odd twist that amused both Anne and her, one reviewer compared the art for *Apples and Pumpkins* to Lois Lenski's. It was about then, too, that Lizzy became a mother.

Like Anne before her, Lizzy was determined to keep working after her son, Nicholas, was born. Anne saw that as a writer she could help. Now she and Lizzy became full-fledged collaborators. "The first books Mom wrote for me were not all that different from the ones she wrote for Dad. *Pots and Pans* (Macmillan, 1993) was a lot like *The Toolbox.*" It was a matter-of-fact book about the everyday things that fascinate small children. Lizzy, meanwhile, was also experimenting. She illustrated *A Nest Full of Eggs* (HarperCollins, 1995), text by Priscilla Belz Jenkins, the first by a writer not connected with her family. Then came *Show & Tell Day* (HarperCollins, 1997), "a story," Lizzy says, "Mom wouldn't have written for Dad or herself. It was the first book she wrote for me."

"When I wrote for Harlow," Anne says, "it was for the child who is spellbound by the magic of everyday things. When I write for myself, I write about one child seeing—the lone child, the one I felt like growing up. But for Lizzy, I write about relationships."

In 1992, Nicholas was having trouble settling in at preschool. Anne wanted to write a book for children in Nicky's situation. She recalls: "We wanted to include children of different cultures and from different kinds of families. We ended up with a cast of ten.

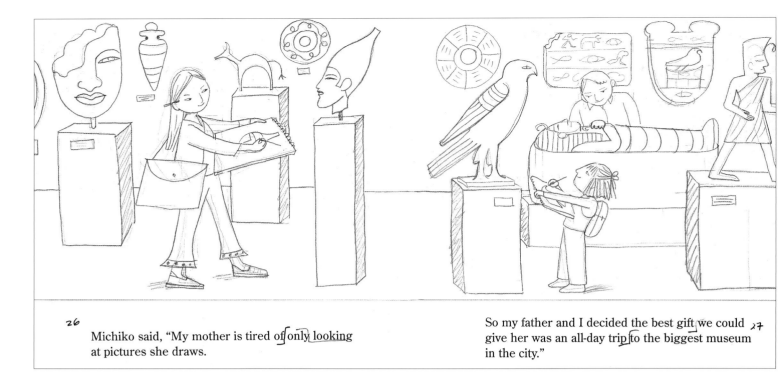

26 Michiko said, "My mother is tired of only looking at pictures she draws.

27 So my father and I decided the best gift we could give her was an all-day trip to the biggest museum in the city."

Dummy drawn in pencil for Mother's Day.

It was like nothing I had ever written! The children became real to us, each with a role. Eveline was the show-off. Evan, the quiet one. Michiko, the artist." Ideas for more books about the children and their families flowed easily: *Halloween Day* (HarperCollins, 1997), *Valentine's Day* (HarperCollins, 2000), *Career Day* (HarperCollins, 2000), *Mother's Day* (HarperCollins, 2004), *Father's Day* (HarperCollins, 2005).

But the writing itself did not come easily to Anne. "The books that look the easiest," she observes, "are often the hardest. Each word has to count and much must be left to the reader's imagination. In any case, I think it's better not to spell out the emotion because the truth is, one child might feel nervous or excited in a given situation and another might not."

For a long time, drawing people did not come easily to Lizzy. "But my feeling for people somehow fed my drawing. The books that my mom and I do together are really about community: about people getting along. They are about how the world should be—and possibly could be."

Does that make the stories unreal? Lizzy wonders about this, but not her mother.

"No," Anne says. "They *are* real because our books are about the world that small children *need* to have."

Children's Books   1350 Avenue of the Americas   Telephone 212-261-6500
New York, New York   Fax 212-261-6689
10019-4703

HarperCollins*Publishers*

13 December 02

Dear Lizzy,

What a great dummy for MOTHER'S DAY! Was it liberating to get to do all those double spreads? We want to make those flower endpapers into wrapping paper or sheets -- a pants pattern that you might find at Putamayo?

In an effort to make it up to you for all those many, many times I've been behind, we met with Elynn in record time so that we could get our comments out to you (in record time).

Anne sent us a lovely e.mail telling us just how much she loves the dummy. I didn't have a chance to talk with her about specifics so in the interest of time and haste, I'll carbon this letter to her so that she's in the loop, too.

One more comment about the spreads. They work beautifully in most all instances. In a few places, where type was boxed in, we've thought of a way to work around it and it will also mean that you won't need to paint a double-spread. More, later.

Jacket	Eveline and Mom? Just Eveline? We never put adults on the cover so just Eveline and her paper button flower? Or for MOTHER'S DAY and FATHER'S DAY, we make an exception and allow for adult on cover?
Front endpapers	Okay, it sounded like such a great idea when we were talking. But somehow, the front endpapers seem somewhat spare compared to the back endpapers. Do you want to use back endpapers for front and back? Or you can add other items the kids use to make the flowers – pipecleaners, leaves, tissue paper, glue etc. for front endpaper.
Title page	Really lovely and perfectly captures a Mother's Day book motif. I'm sure I'm being dense but I'm worried that editorially it doesn't seem to fit in with the rest of the book. I'm assuming Eveline (and mom?) are going to be on the jacket so perhaps we could see them in the front matter. Or just Eveline carrying the breakfast tray. Let's discuss. Could we see revised sketch?

6-7	Love this opening. We love the thermos so much we wondered if you also wanted to give the cereal a name. Add decoration to the side of the lunch box, too? Where are Eveline and mom sitting? At a table or a counter top? Eveline looks like she's kind of high up.
8-9	We will ask Anne if we can two words for more transition from Eveline's breakfast table to school setting, ie "At school….".
10-11	Love it.
12-13	This one is so close. Great to see males working away in the kitchen! Are you sure you want a box for type to obscure that fabulous Martha Stewart kitchen? Perhaps instead of cabinetry, behind Eveline, there's the kitchen wall. This could be a nice open space for type. Or you can give us a soft edge around Eveline, her Dad and her brother to delineate art. Copy still goes above art of Eveline. Let's figure this out together. No need to send revised sketch.
14-15	Love it. Here's where you can tell that I'm no hiker. I asked Elynn if there would be guard rails on the cliff! Maybe the cliff could be just a tad less steep. Don't think you'll need to box in type. It can go right in the sky.
16-17	I know there were so many great ideas to illustrate in Evan's piece. Much as we'd hate to lose anything, I think it could still be very effective if we simplified. As you can probably guess already, we're worried about boxing in the type. Much as I love the double spreads in the book, I think we can have a mix of spreads and pages where we have full bleed, full page art facing all copy. We could try this here. How about expanding the picture of Evan and mom in the backyard? Could we see revised sketch? Copy goes on p.16 and if it were too horrible to lose all the tools, we could have a spot or so to show the birdhouse in progress. It would work fine without spots, too.

A portion of a letter from editor Phoebe W. Yeh to Lizzy with comments on the art for Mother's Day.

Thumbnail sketches drawn in pencil for Mother's Day.

Books in the Family

DONALD CREWS, ANN JONAS, AND NINA CREWS

Crews, Donald. *Carousel*. New York: Greenwillow, 1982.

_____. *Shortcut*. New York: Greenwillow, 1992.

_____. *Truck*. New York: Greenwillow, 1980.

Crews, Nina. *I'll Catch the Moon*. New York: Greenwillow, 1996.

_____. *The Neighborhood Mother Goose*. New York: Amistad/HarperCollins, 2004.

_____. *Snowball*. New York: Greenwillow, 1997.

Jonas, Ann. *Aardvarks, Disembark!* New York: Greenwillow, 1990.

_____. *Bird Talk*. New York: Greenwillow, 1999.

_____. *The Trek*. New York: Greenwillow, 1985.

CLEMENT HURD, EDITH THACHER HURD, AND THACHER HURD

Brown, Margaret Wise. *Bumble Bugs and Elephants*, illustrated by Clement Hurd. New York: William R. Scott, 1938.

Dodds, Dayle Ann. *Wheel Away!*, illustrated by Thacher Hurd. New York: Harper & Row, 1989.

Hurd, Clement. *The Merry Chase*. New York: Random House, 1941.

Hurd, Edith Thacher. *Sandpipers*, illustrated by Lucienne Bloch. New York: Crowell, 1961.

_____. *Wilson's World*, illustrated by Clement Hurd. New York: Harper & Row, 1971.

_____, and Margaret Wise Brown. *Five Little Firemen*, illustrated by Tibor Gergely. New York: Simon & Schuster, 1949.

Hurd, Thacher. *Axle the Freeway Cat*. New York: Harper & Row, 1981.

_____. *Mama Don't Allow*. New York: Harper & Row, 1984.

Stein, Gertrude. *The World Is Round*, illustrated by Clement Hurd. New York: William R. Scott, 1939.

WALTER DEAN MYERS AND CHRISTOPHER MYERS

Cummings, E. E. *Love: Selected Poems by E. E. Cummings*, illustrated by Christopher Myers. New York: Jump at the Sun/Hyperion, 2005.

Hurston, Zora Neale. *Lies and Other Tall Tales*, adapted and illustrated by Christopher Myers. New York: HarperCollins, 2005.

Myers, Christopher. *Fly!* New York: Jump at the Sun/Hyperion, 2001.

————. *Wings*. New York: Scholastic, 2000.

Myers, Walter Dean. *The Blues of Flats Brown*, illustrated by Nina Laden. New York: Holiday House, 2000.

————. *Brown Angels: An Album of Pictures and Verse*. New York: HarperCollins, 1993.

————. *Jazz*, illustrated by Christopher Myers. New York: Holiday House, 2006.

————. *Malcolm X: A Fire Burning Brightly*, illustrated by Leonard Jenkins. New York: HarperCollins, 2000.

————. *Patrol: An American Soldier in Vietnam*, illustrated by Ann Grifalconi. New York: HarperCollins, 2002.

JERRY PINKNEY AND BRIAN PINKNEY

Andersen, Hans Christian. *The Ugly Duckling*, illustrated by Jerry Pinkney. New York: Morrow, 1999.

Lester, Julius, *John Henry*, illustrated by Jerry Pinkney. New York: Dial, 1994.

————. *The Old African*, illustrated by Jerry Pinkney. New York: Dial, 2005.

Pinkney, Andrea Davis. *Duke Ellington: The Piano Prince and His Orchestra*, illustrated by Brian Pinkney. New York: Jump at the Sun/Hyperion, 1998.

Pinkney, Brian. *The Adventures of Sparrowboy*. New York: Simon & Schuster, 1997.

————. *Hush, Little Baby*. New York: Amistad/HarperCollins, 2005.

————. *Max Found Two Sticks*. New York: Simon & Schuster, 1994.

Pinkney, Gloria Jean, ed. *Music from Our Lord's Holy Heaven*, prelude by Troy Pinkney-Ragsdale; illustrated by Jerry Pinkney, Brian Pinkney, and Myles C. Pinkney. New York: Amistad/HarperCollins, 2005.

San Souci, Robert D. *The Faithful Friend*, illustrated by Brian Pinkney. New York: Simon & Schuster, 1995.

HARLOW ROCKWELL, ANNE ROCKWELL, AND LIZZY ROCKWELL

Angelou, Maya. *Maya's World: Angelina of Italy*, illustrated by Lizzy Rockwell. New York: Random House, 2004.

Rockwell, Anne. *Olly's Polliwogs*, illustrated by Harlow Rockwell. New York: Doubleday, 1970.

————. *100 School Days*, illustrated by Lizzy Rockwell. New York: HarperCollins, 2002.

_____. *Only Passing Through: The Story of Sojourner Truth*, illustrated by R. Gregory Christie. New York: Knopf, 2000.

_____. *Paintbrush and Peacepipe: The Story of George Catlin*. New York: Atheneum, 1971.

_____. *Robber Baby: Stories from the Greek Myths*. New York: Greenwillow, 1994.

_____. *Sally's Caterpillar*, illustrated by Harlow Rockwell. New York: Parents Magazine Press, 1966.

Rockwell, Harlow. *Look at This*. New York: Macmillan, 1978.

Rockwell, Lizzy. *Good Enough to Eat: A Kid's Guide to Food and Nutrition*. New York: HarperCollins, 1999.

Witte, Eve, and Pat Witte. *Touch Me Book*, illustrated by Harlow Rockwell. Racine: Golden Press, 1961.

MORE BOOKS ABOUT PICTURE BOOKS

Bang, Molly Garrett. *Picture This: How Picture Books Work*. New York: SeaStar, 2000.

Borden, Louise. *The Journey That Saved Curious George: The True Wartime Escape of Margret and H. A. Rey*; illustrated by Allan Drummond. Boston: Houghton Mifflin, 2005.

Christelow, Eileen. *What Do Authors Do?* New York: Clarion, 1995.

_____. *What Do Illustrators Do?* New York: Clarion, 1999.

Cummings, Pat. *Talking with Artists*. Vol. 1. New York: Bradbury Press, 1992; Vol. 2. New York: Simon & Schuster, 1995; Vol. 3. New York: Clarion, 1999.

Cummins, Julie. *Wings of an Artist: Children's Book Illustrators Talk About Their Art*. New York: Abrams, 1999.

Marcus, Leonard S. *A Caldecott Celebration: Six Artists and Their Paths to the Caldecott Medal*. New York: Walker, 1998.

_____. *The Making of* Goodnight Moon. New York: HarperCollins, 1997.

_____. *Side by Side: Five Favorite Picture-Book Teams Go to Work*. New York: Walker, 2001.

Reading Is Fundamental. *The Art of Reading: Forty Illustrators Celebrate RIF's 40th Anniversary*, foreword by Leonard S. Marcus. New York: Dutton, 2005.

Glossary

Abstract Painting A painting that uses color, line, and form to express attitudes and emotions, instead of realistically depicting people, places, or things.

Art Director A person whose job it is to work with an illustrator to create the overall look of a picture book, advertisement, or other design project.

Calligraphy Handwriting so graceful and fine that it qualifies as art.

Collage Artwork made up of pieces of colored paper, fabric, or other materials, arranged to form a pleasing picture or design.

Dummy A special sketchbook that an illustrator puts together as a first step in deciding what a picture book's finished illustrations will look like and where each picture will go.

Editor The person at a publishing house who offers suggestions for making an author's or illustrator's work better.

Graphic Design The art of creating posters, book jackets, magazine ads, and other images meant to have instant visual appeal while also communicating a useful message.

Handicrafts A wide variety of skilled activities, including weaving, jewelry making, wood carving, and others, that are carried out primarily by hand, and result in the creation of one-of-a-kind objects that are both beautiful and useful.

Medium The raw material used in making an artwork. For example, an artist may draw a picture in the medium of "pencil" or "ink," or make a sculpture in the medium of "clay" or "marble."

Mural A very large artwork, often painted or drawn directly on the wall of a public place such as a courthouse, museum, or library.

Page Layout The overall visual plan for a page, which is decided on after careful thought about how best to balance and blend all the page's individual elements: title, text, and illustrations, among others.

Portfolio A selection of the best examples of an illustrator's work, for use in showing to editors and art directors who might wish to offer the illustrator an assignment.

Publishing Contract A written agreement between a publisher and author or illustrator, stating when a book project is due, how much the publisher will pay for it, and what the author or illustrator needs to provide.

Scratchboard A picture-making technique. The artist starts with a piece of white cardboard that is completely covered with a layer of black wax, chalk, or ink. A sharp tool is used to create a drawing by scratching through the black layer to make lines of contrasting white.

Studio A well-lighted room where an artist or designer works.

Thumbnail Sketch One of a series of rough, small-scale drawings that some artists make as they develop their ideas for a picture book's illustrations.

Type The letter forms, number forms, and other characters needed for printing a text. Type comes in a great many styles, each with a distinctive look and personality.

Watercolor A kind of artist's paint that is made ready for use by mixing it with water. Illustrations made with this medium often have a delicate, transparent quality.

Index

NOTE: Page numbers in italics refer to illustrations.